TRANSFORM
YOURSELF FROM AN
INDIVIDUAL
CONTRIBUTOR TO A
GROUP
LEADER
AND MORE...

TRANSFORM
YOURSELF FROM AN
INDIVIDUAL
CONTRIBUTOR TO A
GROUP
LEADER
AND MORE...

N K SINGH

WhiteFalcon
Publishing

www.whitefalconpublishing.com

Transform Yourself from Individual Contributor
to Group Leader and More...
N K Singh

www.whitefalconpublishing.com

ISBN - 978-93-87193-74-1

Who will need this Book?

You need this book if answer to any of the below question is **"YES"** from you.

Are you tired of working as an individual contributor and wants to be a Team Leader, Manager and more in your future roles?

Would you like to be a Team Leader or Manager of your Team right after a year or two from now?

Is your promotion to Team Leader or Managerial role stuck due to office politics?

Do you want to be promoted after every year or at least after two years in your job?

Do you have a desire to be a corporate leader in your career going forward?

Are you a fresh Management or Engineering graduate who wants to be a distinguished employee from day one in professional life and wants to get quick professional and personal success in future?

Are you a project manager or delivery head or head of an organization who wants to increase his or her team performance 50% more by aligning your workforce with the purpose of your organization?

About the Author

The author of this book Mr. N K Singh is a professional in information technology industry. He holds two master's degrees on the name of formal education, one in the field of computer science and another one in the field of management. He started his career as an engineer and after having 3 years of industry experience he started following the principles mentioned in this book to transform himself from individual contributor to a group leader and more. He got tremendous success by following these principles. He worked in many multinational information technology services providing companies as a team leader, manager and senior manager. Only at 12 years of formal working experience in IT industry he joined a multinational information technology services providing company as director operations. The principles and suggestions of this books are the ones he followed in his career to transform himself into a leader. He wants to share them so that the current generation and generation next can be benefited out of it.

The principles mentioned in this book can be applied in any industry or any business domain or work domain and will be very helpful for the transformation of individual contributor role working people into leaders.

Contents

Purpose of this Book

The purpose of this book is to transform individual contributors into group leaders and more going forward in future so that they can add more values to the organization they are working for, to the society the they are living in, to the family they are part of and above all to their own personal life. This transformation is important because after working for five plus years, a person gets very good competency and experience in his or her concerned work domain and starts giving best contribution to his or her working organization in his or her best individual capacity. But at this stage only that best individual capacity contribution is not expected to be enough by the organization where the best individual contribution giving person is working. At this stage (stage where a person has 5+ years of work experience) an organization expects experienced people to take good initiatives to make things better in organization and take their fellow colleagues together in whatever they are doing on the name of professional work improvements. They are also expected to make their colleagues especially less experienced ones to perform at their level best by training them, mentoring them, coaching them, guiding them and motivating them. Besides execution of routine work; organizations have these enhanced expectations from experienced people because experienced people are facilitated more in terms of salary, bonus etc.

On one hand organizations have the above said expectations and on the other hand experienced people in individual contributor role do not known these expectations or even if they know these expectations, they do not know how to meet these expectations. Due to this gap between expectations and responses against them, both the organization and experienced people in individual contributor role; happen to be disappointed a lot with each other. Organization is disappointed because it does not get the results expected from experienced individual contributors and experienced individual contributors are disappointed because they are not facilitated as per their experience in terms of salary hike, bonus and promotion because they do not meet the organization expectations.

This book will help all such experienced individual contributors by educating them with proven and different ways of working, behaving and living so that they can meet the above said expectation and get their own expectations (good salary hike, good bonus and promotion on faster basis) fulfilled year on year.

Besides that, this book will also help ambitious fresh management or engineering graduates who want to be distinguished employees from day one at work and want to get quick success year on year.

This book will very helpful to project managers, head of departments or head of organizations if they feel that their manpower is not aligned with their purpose and that's why their productivity is not enough. In this case they will have to make their manpower read this book to get them motivated enough to be aligned with the end purpose of the organization and deliver their best as per the organization purpose. This book will help in transforming individual contributors into leaders and this transformation process takes around 2 years of time. During this entire transformation process, the undergoing people happen to be highly motivated, well behaved, innovative and high performing employees. Such attitude of employees gives tremendous positive results to organizations. Once this transformation is complete, organizations get many people leaders, technology leaders and business domain or work domain leaders as valuable employees.

This book will help in achieving the above said objectives by transforming people into leaders. When I say leaders, I mean not only people leaders but also technology leaders or domain leaders. Many people think leadership as a people management role only and they don't want to be leaders because they are technology, or a business domain or work domain lovers and they look for their career in complex and challenging job responsibilities as senior employees in their interested technology or business domain or work domain. Leadership is not limited to people management only. It is applied in technology management, business domain management or a work domain management as well and in today's world there are job roles to do this. Few examples of such roles are technology architect, Consultant, finance manager, risk manager, business analyst, technical lead, technology manager, technology director, chief technology officer etc. So, people who wants to be in such roles in their future, they also will have to transform themselves as leaders because they will have to lead a group of people by educating them, mentoring them, guiding them and even motivating them so that they can work as per their (of the domain or technology experts) expectations to achieve the end objectives of the organization. This way this book will be helpful to those who wants to be people leader or technology leader or domain leader in their future roles.

Introduction

In this book I will talk about five mantras (principles) that need to be followed by all who wants to transform themselves from individual contributor to group leader and more going forward. These mantras were practised by me from the very early days of my professional life and the results were very prosperous in terms of my fast career development and my overall professional growth.

I started my career as an engineer in IT industry and during my first three years of professional working as an individual contributor I observed that who so ever was doing something different, something unique and something value adding besides his or her routine work; was getting benefitted quickly in terms of good salary hike, promotion, better role and responsibilities assignments etc. Those three years I kept observing and kept collecting all the different, unique and value adding actions being done by my more experienced colleagues. Though the number of such colleagues were very few but the outcome they were getting was tremendous. I also wanted to avail all those tremendous benefits that's why I started practising all the activities that I had observed and collected. I started practising them when I was a three-year experienced IT professional and right after two years when I was having five years of experience; I was promoted as Team Leader in my organization. I delivered excellent results as Team Leader in next three years and then I joined a different organization as a manager. In my job change and role change (from team leader to manager), execution of all those observed and collected activities played a big role. Because their execution gave me so much of professional competency, knowledge, confidence, vision for the future and ability to make strategy and its execution capability that I not only easily cleared my selection interview but also justified my new role at my new organization. At my new organization I practised the same old set of observed and collected activities along with few new ones that I had observed during my days working as team leader. Again, I got benefited in terms of a promotion as a senior manager. This happened to me right after a year of joining my organization as a manager. I worked for this organization as senior manager for three years and then I changed my job again as a director operation in a IT MNC.

Now after 14 years of my professional career (from an engineer to director operation) I observed many activities working for professionals very positively and I also practised them and got benefitted a lot. As mentioned earlier I also kept collecting all such activities and made them part of my professional tool kit. In this book I have grouped all such activities in five different bundles and I call them "Five mantras for transformation from individual contributor to group leader and more". These mantras are fully tested and experienced hypothesis for me and I recommend all individual contributors, fresh management or engineering graduates to practice them with full faith to have tremendous success in their life.

Have a decisive Day in Your Life

I know that you are in a hurry to learn the five mantras for your transformation from individual contributor to group leader and more, but I will strongly recommend you go over this chapter first. This chapter will lay a strong mental foundation in you to understand those five mantras properly and to practice them in your professional life. The main purpose of this chapter is to explain you the future life of yours as a leader in terms of how a leader should live, behave, work, handle situation etc. so that you can assess yourself and take a decision whether you will be able to meet those future expectations as leader or not. If think you will not be able to meet those expectations, then I will recommend you a different career path as an individual contributor because without meeting those expectations you will never be a successful leader.

I am emphasizing a lot on this chapter and understanding of the future expectations that will be associated with you if you become a leader because many people decide to become leader just by getting impressed with the rosy side of leader's life. By rosy side of leader's life, I mean the facilities and privileges that a leader gets like separate office space, flexibility of office time, many company given facilities etc... All these things are given to leaders so that they can do their work efficiently but there is other side of leader's life as well that many people do not know but a would-be leader should know that very well so that the would-be leader can take a decision whether to be a leader or not.

Spend a day and think HONESTLY on below conditions that a leader faces every day and take a decision whether you would like to be a leader or not. If you are fine with these conditions or you are sure that you will develop yourself to cope up with these conditions, then you can proceed with the practice of the five mantras for your transformation but if you think that neither you are fine with these conditions nor you think you will be in a position to develop yourself in future to cope up with these conditions then you should not try for leadership career and you should look for something in individual contributor role only.

Below are the conditions you must take a decision on:

❖ *Are you a people loving person?* A leader has to be a very good people loving person. He or She has to enjoy dealing with people. People working with him or her as colleagues, working under him or her as sub-ordinates, people leader himself or herself is working under and people you as a leader are supposed to serve as customers. So, if you want to be a leader then you will have to be a people loving person that means you will have to like dealing with people first and you will have to know the skills of dealing with different type of people in different situations. Please take a self-decision here whether you would like to be that kind of person or not if your answer is yes then please proceed further. In case you think that you will not be able to be this kind of a person then please step back and try your other individual contributor career options.

❖ *Are you ready to take a hit on yourself for other's mistakes?* A leader is accountable for his or her team Success or failures. When the team succeeds, the leader should give all credits to his or her team but when the team fails, the leader should take full responsibility on himself or herself. This is the rule of accountability of a leader. It works like that because a leader is facilitated with everything to get the job done successfully by his or her team, so something is not working as expected then the leader should be vigilant enough to detect that and take actions before it can cause a total failure. So, if total failure occurs, the leader should take the full accountability of the same. But at the time of success the leader should give full credit to his or her team for the success because this action will further motivate the team and they will bring few more successes in future. Your team will feel cheated if you as a leader take full credit for the success and they will not do their best from next project onwards. They will feel so because they are the actual doer of the work and your job as a leader is just to co-ordinate, solve problems, taking care of deadlines etc… that is also not easy but not as tough as the execution of the actual work.

As a leader your job is to bring success after success in your organization by keeping your team motivated for the great achievements, so I strongly recommend you follow this principle. Now if you feel that you as a would-be leader will not be able to cope up with this situation or you do not like handling this situation in this way then please do not proceed for your leadership career.

I know it is very hard to believe the rule of accountability of a leader, but this is how a true leadership role goes. One thing you as a would-be leader needs to understand very clearly that your job is to keep your team motivated at all costs that is possible on the ground of your organization policy, law of the land, humanity and spirituality overall. If you do it successful, then you will always be successful as a leader.

To make you understand the rule of accountability of a leader, I will narrate a story of a key Indian Government project that **Dr. A.P.J Abdul Kalam** (The great Indian scientist and former president of India) was leading and the project failed. Dr Kalam himself narrated this story many times in his conference speeches while addressing failures in life as a leader.

In 1979 Dr. A.P.J Abdul Kalam was project director in ISRO and his project was to put a satellite in orbit using SLV3 (Satellite launching vehicle 3). Everything went well in preparation and finally the launching day came. The launching procedure was started, and the launching clock time started coming down. When launch time reached less than a minute, the computer that was handling the launching data displayed error "Don't launch". Immediately around six scientists who were sub-ordinates of Dr. Kalam analysed the error and all related systems and they came up with an opinion that the error was coming because there was fuel leakage in the control system, but the launch could proceed as there was sufficient fuel for the launch. Based on his sub-ordinates feedbacks Dr. Kalam decided to launch the satellite by passing the computer error. The satellite was launched and after some time it fell into the Bay of Bengal instead of going to the orbit. This way the satellite launch got failed.

Outside the launch site there was a press conference scheduled to update the status to the country. Those days ISRO (Indian Space Research Organization) was being headed by Prof Satish Dhawan who was chairman of ISRO. Prof Dhawan went to the Dr. Kalam and asked him to come for the press conference. While going for the press conference Dr. Kalam was very afraid and he was sure that he would be made scapegoat for the failure because he was the project director. But nothing like that happened. Instead, Prof Dhawan addressed the press conference and took all the questions. In the end he assured the press that next year the same team will succeed because it was a very good team in his opinion. After this failure there were many criticisms for ISRO, but Prof Dhawan managed all by taking everything on himself. Next year in July 1980 the same satellite launch was tried by the same team and this time everything went well. After the successful launch Prof Dhawan went to Dr. Kalam and asked him to go alone and take the press conference.

The main take way of this story is the rule of accountability of a leader that we discussed above. This is what rule of self-accountability for leader is all about.

❖ *Are you fine with being in last of the beneficiary list of your group?* Leadership is a people's service that's why a leader should first benefit others (sub-ordinates & customers) and then the leader is benefited automatically. A leader success is measured by his or her team success, so a leader should empower his or her team to be successful. If you are fine with this approach of leadership then please proceed with this book further because when you will be leader and you do not practice this approach, then you will not be successful as a leader. Instead if you think that you are not fine with this approach then you should better try your career luck in individual contributor roles.

❖ *Are you fine with being people's servant as a leader?*
A leader has to serve (Not to rule) his or her people to make a difference in their life. This service is a continuous process to understand people's problems and solve them, to enable and empower them more and more and to give them more conducive environment to enable them to deliver more against their goals. I would like to emphasize on this quality of a leader because many people believe that leadership role is a licence to rule over their subordinates, but this approach of leadership is not liked by people and they deliver their least while working under such leaders. By least delivery I mean the minimum delivery needed to save the job and to get the salary. Instead leadership is an opportunity to serve people by bringing a difference in their life. When people feel that their leader is bringing a difference in their life then only they do their best against the goals set for them by their leader.

    Now if you think that you will be able to work as per this model of leadership then you can proceed with this book further otherwise there is no use because without this approach you will not be a successful leader.

❖ *Are you fine with bringing more skilled and knowledgeable people in your team?* A leader has to recruit more skilled and knowledgeable people than himself or herself in his or her team. This is needed because whatever the leader knows is already an asset of the organization and the organization is already getting benefits out of it. But if a leader gets more skilled and knowledgeable candidates during the selection process and does not recruit them under the impression that the candidates are more qualified than himself or herself then the leader will never be successful as a leader. As stated earlier that a leader success is measured by the success of his or her team. The more skilled and knowledgeable team the leader has, the more will be the level of success of the leader. A leader should not keep himself or herself only as the most skilled or knowledgeable person in his or her team instead he or she should bring more skilled or more knowledgeable people than himself or herself. A leader has to channelize the competency of his or her great team to achieve greater results.

Here you will have to clear your head that you will have to follow this approach when you will be leader in future so please take a call right now whether you will be able to do so or not. If not, then you should try for your career progress as individual contributor.

❖ *Are you fine with delegating some of your responsibilities to your right below level sub-ordinates?* The leader who is ALWAYS busy in doing his or her assigned works; is not supposed to be leader and should look for career opportunities as individual contributor. A leader must have some free time out of his or her busy schedule to do some development works considering future changes in mind. A leader should be ready for the future changes that comes in organization, business domain, technology, political situation etc. But if a leader is always occupied in his or her routine works then he or she will not get time to anticipate such changes and to make strategy to cope up with those changes. Some of such changes can be great opportunities for the leader or for the organization overall but due to full indulgence in back to back routine work the leader might miss that opportunity. That's why a leader has to be good at delegating his or her streamlined responsibilities (possible ones) to his or her sub-ordinates. He or she should also groom some of the sub-ordinates for his or her own role considering future in mind because in future if the leader is promoted further then there should be someone well trained to fill his or her position immediately. Many leaders do not do it as they are afraid that their sub-ordinates will take over their own role. Let me tell you that it does not work this way in business organization. If you groom and make your subordinates ready for your own role then your chances of further promotions are high because your this attitude as a leader is liked by business organizations. Such delegations and grooming make the shoulder of leader a bit light because the leader passes down some of his or her responsibilities to his or her subordinates. This way the leader gets some free time and utilizes this free time to be ready for the future changes.

Now if you do not agree with this approach of leadership then please do not proceed further on this book and also you should not try your career progress in leadership role. You should be fine as individual contributor.

As a would-be leader it's time to take the final decision on your career now. So just last time have a look at all the conditions that we discussed so far and take a final decision whether you agree with all these conditions or not. If you agree then please proceed with my five mantras that will start from next chapter onwards. In case you disagree with any of the conditions then please close this book here only and look for better career opportunities in individual contributor role only.

1ˢᵗ *Mantra* ————————————

"First be the one that you want to make others"

Now as you are well determined to become a leader in future as part of your professional career, you should start learning and practising all my five mantras one by one starting with this first one.

You will never want people with bad qualities working under you when you will be a leader. It is a common human nature that everyone wants to have ideal sub-ordinates because working with them is easy and fruitful. In case of any issue with subordinates, leaders quickly give advice to bring changes in behaviour, attitude, communication etc. Similarly, sub-ordinates also want to work under an ideal leader so that their professional and personal life can be progressive and fruitful. So, if you want to be a leader you need to be an ideal person and professional first before you expect your subordinates to be an ideal person and professional. In your case you need to be ideal a person and professional first for your colleagues because you are not a leader now and you do not have any subordinates who work under you. So, you will have to start shaping yourself as an ideal professional and person now so that your colleagues can trust on you, want to support you on whatever you do and want to become like you as a professional or as a person. When you do it (try being ideal), you will be observed by your own leaders and you will be in the limelight in your organization. This way you will be benefitted in your organization in many ways. The day you become an ideal professional and person for your colleagues, your first step of becoming a leader will be successful. Because for a leader preaching and practice should be same. A leader should preach the same thing that he or she is practising in his or her own personal or professional life. If there is a difference between preaching and practice then people (Subordinates, colleagues etc.) are not going to buy the leader's preaching. In this case it will be very difficult for the leader to win the trust of his or her people and get any work completed with superb results and it will be very difficult for the leader to manage his or her people as well because the people will not trust the leader at all. Certainly, there will be difference between preaching and practice of a leader if the leader is not an ideal professional or person in his or her own professional or personal life. But if you yourself is an ideal professional or person now and become a leader in future then you will get tremendous support and trust from your subordinates because that time your preaching and practice will be same, and this sameness is liked by subordinates or followers.

For a long time, we are talking about ideal professional, ideal person or ideal leader so let's discuss what defines an ideal professional or ideal leader. Below are the commonly liked qualities in business, sports, education, social services or any work culture of the world and a person having these qualities are called ideal professional, ideal person or ideal employee. So, develop them in yourself at your best and demonstrate them on every occasion in your personal or professional life. So that people having these qualities get attracted towards you and like to be in your circle as your colleagues or as your subordinates and then you can make progress towards fulfilling your desire of becoming a leader in future. Carve one thing in your mind very clearly that only ideal person and professional is given opportunity to become a leader. Even if non-ideal person and professional becomes a leader by chance then he or she will be unsuccessful for sure as a leader. So, start developing all these below qualities in yourself at your level best.

❖ *Passion*: An ideal person, professional or leader should be passionate for whatever he or she does. So, follow your passion and be EXTREMELY passionate for whatever you do as a profession. If you are not in a profession where your passion is then please change your profession soon because you are not going to be progressive in that profession. Passion and profession of a person should be same to be highly successful in life because that sameness will make you do your best in that profession. This way you will be a very high productive person, professional or leader and you will be getting success against your high productivity. On the other hand, if your profession is not your passion then you will not be highly productive and will be doing just the bare minimum so that you can get just life essential benefits only to survive. This way you will block your own success. Because our personal and professional environment follows a simple rule "If you do not deliver more against your personal and professional responsibilities then you will not be delivered more in your own personal and professional life in terms of success, happiness, respect, self-satisfaction etc.". So please choose your profession as per your passion but whatever profession you choose for yourself, please make sure that is legally, spiritually and socially acceptable.

To make you understand the importance of passion for success in life let me briefly narrate the story of ***Nike Shoes founder Mr. Bill Bowerman.*** Bill was a science teacher in US in a high school and this was his only source of income. He was having passion for sports specially athletics but being married man he was unable to go after his passion. After few years he took a decision to go after his passion together with his job and he left his current job as a science teacher and joined another school as a sports teacher on a low salary than his previous job. At his new job as a sports teacher he worked very hard and made a very good team of athletes ready within a year. As a result, that school performed very well in some district level and state level games. This spread the popularity of Bill as a school level sports coach. Due to this popularity he got opportunity to be sports coach at a university in US. At his university job he again made a very good team of athletes ready in a very short span of time. Those athletes performed very well in state and national level games. This further intensified the popularity of Bill and he became very famous as a sports coach in US. As an advantage his got opportunities to groom many good athletes and he groomed them very well leaving his university job. Those athletes did superb at national and international level games. Few of them did very well in Olympics as well. Now Bill was very popular athletics coach in US and enjoying his success. But he was not satisfied with the design of the athletics sports shoes being manufactured by all the shoe manufacturing companies. He was having his own design blue print and was approaching each sports shoe manufacturing companies to manufacture shoes as per that. Because he was having justification for the athletes improved performance after wearing his new design shoes. But in the end, he could not convince even a single shoe making company to accept his design. Then Bill contacted one very small shoe manufacturer and got few shoes manufactured only for few of his athletes. Those athletes did very well in their next games wearing the new design shoes. Their enhanced performance further consolidated the belief of Bill and he decided to set up his own sports shoe manufacturing company. He made few of his athletes invest in his company to manage required finances and set up a company called "Blue Ribbon". This company grew a lot and became "Nike" after few years.

Now you can understand the power of actions based on one's passion. In this example, actions against one's passion created many good athletes at national and international level. It also created an international sports wear manufacturing brand.

So, if you want to be an ideal person or an ideal professional or an ideal leader then you should chase your passion because your success lies there only. There might be situations restricting you from going after your passion but try to take some wise decisions like Bill so that you can better manage all those situations and your passion as well. Also keep in mind that even after reaching the peak of your success you should still be passionate about your work and you should work on things you are passionate about.

Many people don't know their passion because some of them never cared for it and some of them are good at more than one or two things in life and enjoy dealing with all that's why they don't know which one their passion is. I would like to give a key advice for such people to find out their passion.

Step 1 - Please write 5 things in descending order of priority that you are good at.

Step 2 - choose at least 3 things from above list that excite you from within or you enjoy doing that. Arrange them in descending order of priority. I mean what you like most should be at the top and the least should be the last.

Step 3 - Do some research and find out which one is having better growth opportunities at present and in future as well. Again, arrange them in descending order of priority. Keep the highest opportunity one at the top and the lowest at the end of your list.

Step 4 - Choose any of top two from your list and the selected thing is your passion.

The above mentioned 4 steps will make your profession aligned with your passion.

Now as you know your passion so it's time to put your head, heart and hands all together with best of your capacity to pursue it as a profession to have abundance of everything in your life.

❖ *Punctuality:* An ideal person or an ideal professional or an ideal leader should be punctual in his or her time commitments. Whether you have to complete a work, or you have to attend a meeting, or you have to reply a customer mail or anything else within a timeline, please keep your promised time commitments. Because delay by anyone due to any reason is not liked globally. So, at time of giving time commitments, you must be very careful of the possibility of its compliance. If you feel that the given time is not enough then you must request for more time span in the very beginning by giving your rationale. However, there might be situations when you will not be able to fulfil your time commitments due to some problems or the other. On those occasions you should inform all required people as early as possible so that they can be aware of the delay in advance. This is needed because no one likes to hear the failure of time commitment at the very last moment.

To be punctual get up every day early in the morning before sunrise and finish your daily routine activities.

Then spend 10-15 minutes of time alone and prepare your personal and professional "to do lists" for the day. "To do list" is just a list of actions that you have to complete for the day. You can use a small note book to write your to do list. After writing every action item don't forget to assign a priority to it by writing a single alphabet key word (High = H, Medium = M, Low = L) at the beginning of each action item. This priority assignment will help you understand which action item needs to be taken care first and which should be the last. Once your to do list is complete then get ready to start your day. After reaching your workplace, have a look at your do list for the day and start working on the action items one by one as per their priority. The high priority ones should be addressed first followed by medium priority ones and the low priority ones should be the last ones to be actioned. Once you complete an action item then either put a cross or tick mark against that action item in your notebook so that you can remember which one is complete and which one is left. If you could not complete an action item due to any reason, then make sure it is in your next day to do list as a high priority action item. This whole life cycle of to do list should be part of your daily life. This to do list is very effective in managing the daily action items. Daily action items mean the action item that can be completed in a day or two. It will not be effective in managing action items that will be completed in a week or month time. To manage long duration action items, you can use an action item tracker. An action item tracker is also a list of action items with few more additional details like planned completion date, responsible person for completion etc. This tracker can be made using a tool like Microsoft excel and can be kept as a soft copy on your computer. You should enter all long duration action items in this tracker and you should also follow them up at least twice in a week so that there can be timely progress against each of them. Action item tracker will be very effective in managing long duration tasks of yours and it will ensure its timely completion on most of the occasions. In case of delay for any action item, at least you will get to know in advance that the concerned action item is getting delayed. Individual action item of action item tracker can be broken down into multiple daily action items and can be part of your daily to do list. This way both these tools will be used to make sure timely delivery against most of your responsibilities. I recommend you to use both these tools (To do list and Action Items Tracker) to improve and maintain your punctuality in your professional as well as personal life. Below is sample action item tracker:

AI Tracker								
Action Item No.	Action Item Details	Status	Priority	Received Date	Assigned To	Actions Taken	Expected Closure Date	Actual Closure Date
1								
2								
3								

If you are supposed to attend a meeting, then try to be five minutes early at the place of the meeting so that you can settle down properly before the meeting starts. Besides that, before 30 minutes of the meeting start time, stop whatever you are doing and prepare yourself for the meeting for the things like, what points you have to discuss in the meeting, what points other people can raise to you, what should be your ideal answer to those points etc. Organize all these things in your mind and on paper in terms of short notes before entering the meeting room. This kind of preparations together with punctuality will make you effective and productive in the meeting and you will be accepted as an ideal person and professional after couple of such meetings.

You can have a look at the life story of any successful person in any field of life and you will find one thing very common that most of them are or were very punctual with their time commitments. So, you should always try to be punctual with your time commitments as it is one of the important quality of an ideal person, professional, leader or would be leader.

❖ **Honesty & Integrity:** This is the most important qualities of an ideal person, professional or a leader. If you want to be an ideal, then you will have to be honest in all your actions while dealing with people around you. At the same point of time you need to be a person who complies with the socially, legally, organizationally, nationally and internationally acknowledged principles. If you as a leader or a would-be leader preaches honesty and integrity all the time but when it comes to their self-compliance, then you lag behind. In that case your subordinates or colleagues are never going to accept you as an ideal leader or ideal colleague or an ideal professional. Honesty and integrity is the foundation on which great building of successful leader is built over a period of time. So, try to lay it as strong as you can because the stronger it will be built the more stronger will be your chances of being successful as a leader if you are a leader already or your chances of becoming a leader will be more stronger if you want to be a leader in future. Because no one wants sub-ordinates who is not honest or a person without integrity and no one wants to work with a leader who is not honest or a person without integrity.

There are some big multinational companies that can bear with underperforming employees for a year, but they cannot bear with an employee even for a day if there is honesty or integrity issue/s. There are many examples where even CEOs of companies have been fired from their jobs due to honesty and integrity issues. Here I don't want to name those companies and CEOs just to avoid some unnecessary controversies. But if you want to know then you can search on internet and you will get to know many.

The purpose of sharing CEOs firing from job news is not to scare you but instead it is to make you understand how important honesty and integrity is for your success as a leader or to become a leader. Now you understand the true importance of honesty and integrity so never compromise on them at all in your life.

As a professional you need to be honest and a person with integrity with your responsibilities. Whatever your responsibilities are you need to deliver against them honestly while taking care of your organization's policies and processes. Besides that, there are many organizational policies related to employee's behaviour at work place, information security etc.so if you want to be an ideal person, professional, leader or you want to be a leader in future then you will have to be extremely good at your compliance to those policies. Because non-followers of policies are nowhere taken as ideal people and people who are not ideal can never be a leader in future or if they happen to be a leader by chance then their success as a leader is impossible. The reason is very simple, you keep your surroundings as per your own likes and dislikes. So, a leader who himself or herself does not follow policies will attract similar kind of people in his organization and those kinds of people will ensure the leader failure and organization failure soon. Because organization policy or process says something to done in a manner and the leader and his or her subordinates would be doing that in a different manner. This way department and organization goals will never be achieved and department or organization or both will fail in next some time. So, if you want to be a leader then be honest with your responsibilities and be a policy compliant person all the time so that you can be taken as an ideal person and be given opportunity to take leadership role in future.

I will give you an example to explain you why people who are honest and a person with integrity are liked in organizations or anywhere else. Imagine there is a family of 5 people father, mother and their 3 children (2 sons and 1 daughter). Father is the head of the family and is loving to all his children, but he will be more inclined towards the one who is honest and a person with integrity when it comes to the compliance of family values and tradition. That's what happens in an organization, the head of a team or division or the head of the organization is loving to all the people working with him or her but he or she is more inclined to those who are honest and people with integrity when it comes to the compliance of given responsibilities, organization policies, organization vision, organization mission and organization values. As a result of this kind of inclination, those special people (honest and people with integrity) enjoy quite a different growth opportunity in the organization. This happens in all the organizations in all part of the world. So, if you want to be successful as a person or if you want to be a leader in your organization or any other organization in future then you will have to be an honest and a person with integrity when it comes to the compliance of organization processes and policies. So please understand your organization policies and processes properly and keep your behaviour and way of working accordingly under any circumstances. This will help you becoming an ideal person and professional.

❖ *High performance:* A leader is expected to deliver high performance by his or her team. The leader will not be able to do this if he or she has not been a high performer in his or her own career as an individual contributor. Because such a leader lacks many good qualities needed to deliver or get high performance delivered. When a person delivers high performance or tries to deliver high performance some qualities get developed in his or her personality by default. These qualities are ability to understand expected goals and delivery, time management, ability to work under pressure, multitasking, collaboration and competency in a particular domain/s. These are the basic qualities needed by a leader in order to get high performance delivered by his or her team. So, if you want to be a leader then you will have to be a high performer in your current role so that you can be ready with the above mentioned qualities and you can be taken as an ideal person or professional in your team and organization. As mentioned earlier and I would like to remind you again that only ideal person and professional is given opportunities for leadership positions so if you want to be a leader in future then you will have to be an ideal person and professional first in your current role. So, to become a leader you will have to be a high performer in your current role and will have to possess qualities like ability to understand expected goals and delivery, time management, ability to work under pressure, multitasking, collaboration and competency in a particular domain/s so that you can utilize them in getting high performance from your team when you will get leadership role in future. But if you are not having these qualities then you will not be able to become a leader or even if you become by chance then you will not be able to deliver high performance as a leader due to lack of these qualities and you will be stamped as an unsuccessful leader. In either case your personal career will have a setback so be a high performer in your present individual contributor role and be all set to be successful in future as a leader. In order to be a high performer please understand your goals very clearly. At the same time, you should also understand the vision, mission, policies, processes and values of your organization very well. Feel free to take help your manager and HR to have this understanding in place. Never ever have any confusion around them because they are the needles of your compass to give you direction for your way of working, living, communicating and behaving in your organization. Now you know your dos and don'ts so push yourself at the best of your capacity accordingly so that you can deliver high performance as per the expectations of your organization.

❖ *Team Work:* This is one of the core qualities of a leader. For a leader entire group of people that is working under him or her; matters. The leader will be successful only when individuals from his or her group of people work with each other with a feeling and attitude of togetherness, collaboration, helping each other, co-existence, common end objective and respect for each other, respect for the leader and the organization overall. The overall performance of the team; defines the performance of the leader and the team cannot give overall good performance if individuals of the team are not having the above said feeling and attitude. Besides that, the leader himself or herself needs to have that feeling and attitude because the team follows the leader. So, each individual of a team needs to be a very good team player. Individual working together with a feeling and attitude mentioned above is called a team player. When many team players work together then the efforts made collectively is called team work. For the success of a team; team work is very important. So, the leader of the team should himself or herself first surrender the feeling of "I will win" and arouse the feeling of "We will win". Then the leader should push each individual of his or her team to have this kind of feeling. Having this feeling must be mandatory for each individual of the team including the leader so that they can work together as per the above-mentioned feeling and attitude and deliver against the common objective/s of the team. If attitude of team work is missing from a team then the team can never be successful. Because each individual of the team will be doing things only for self-benefits without caring for others and even the end objective/s of the team. In absence of respect for others there will be a war like situation in the team all the time. This way the team will miss the end objective/s and the individuals will also miss their individual objectives because it is the proven rule of the world that any great objective cannot be achieved alone as there will always be dependency on others for something or the other. But in a team without team work attitude, helping each other factor will be missing completely. Moreover, in an organization or team, achieving team goal or organization goal is considered first then achievements against individual goals are looked at. If you as an individual achieves your goals but your team or organization misses out the end goal, then your individual achievement will not be considered as valuable as it should have been if your team or organization end goal had been achieved. This way at the end both team members and the team will be unsuccessful because team will miss the end goal and will not be benefitted or facilitated and when team is not benefitted or facilitated then there is no question of the benefits or facilitations of the individual team members.

In the game of soccer, scoring a goal against the opposition team is the primary expectations of all stakeholders of the team. Who scored the goal is the secondary information stakeholders are interested in. So, it should be the responsibility of entire team to play in such a way so that each of them contributes towards making the team winner rather making himself or herself winner. If a forward position player is running with the ball but he is a little far from the goal post than his fellow player who is a bit closer, then he should pass the ball quickly to his fellow player so that he can score a goal for the team. Because when the team will be the winner only then team players will be winner and will be given their required facilitations. This should be the attitude of each and every member of the team and the leader of the team should be a great sponsor and custodian of this attitude.

If you want to be a leader in future, then you will have to be a great team player with attitude of team work. So, by your way of working and behaviour, every moment set examples of togetherness, collaboration, helping each other, co-existence, common end objective and respect for each other, respect for your leader and the organization overall. If you are a leader already then you should enforce such an attitude in your team or in your organization with the help of your organization values. Now a day nearly all organizations have values to enforce team work attitude, so the leader must take help of such organization values to make team work as an organizational culture.

❖ *Supreme Knowledge:* As you know that to become a leader in your future role, you will have to be an ideal person and professional in your current role. So, to be an ideal person and professional you will have to satisfy one condition that is to acquire supreme knowledge in your work domain. You need to be a highly knowledgeable person of your work domain so acquire at least more than double knowledge of your work knowledge requirements. This way you will have an edge over your fellow colleagues and you will be in a position to help them whenever they will need some insight in a situation. Your this kind of help will be appreciated by your colleagues and they will start taking you as a distinguished senior colleague in terms of knowledge and experience. This way your road towards future role of leadership will take a shape at least from your fellow's colleagues acceptance of your superiority of knowledge perspective. Besides that, your leaders will also come to know about your superior knowledge and they will also start taking you as a distinguished team member with supreme knowledge. Both these acceptances will position you at a good place in the queue of future leaders of your organization.

To enhance your knowledge as per the above requirements you will have to take the task of your knowledge management in your own hands. Because such level of knowledge can never be enhanced by your team given or organization given trainings. Team given, or organization given trainings are mainly as per the business needs of the organization and they are given at the required time only. That's why if you want to keep your knowledge more than double of your colleague's knowledge then you will have to take the charge of your knowledge management in your own hands.

Few suggestions to make this happen:

1- Prepare list of items you are supposed to know as part of your work domain and rate your current knowledge level against each of them as Excellent, High, Medium and low.

2- Write a self-study plan against each of item where your knowledge level is less than excellent. Your plan should be to raise your level from low to medium and medium to high.

3- Execute your self-study plan on daily basis without any fail. If anything is not getting clear by self-study then consult any of your senior, refer forums or other relevant materials on internet but try to clarify that.

4- Review your plan on weekly basis and adjust your efforts on the basis of progress made.

5- After completion of self-study you will feel the need of some short-term courses against few of the items. Please plan them on your own expenses as per your convenience but do it as soon as possible because you are making an investment in your career enhancement that will give your 5 times more return when you will be at your next level.

Repeat these 5 steps till the time your knowledge level is not excellent against each item of your work domain. Please keep in mind that when sub-ordinates have any problem, then they approach their leader to take help or to get solution. So, if the leader himself or herself is not knowledgeable enough to help his or her subordinates then the team will not be successful and as a result the leader will not be successful at all. That's why if you want to be a successful leader in your future role then enhance your knowledge up to a great extent in your work domain.

❖ *Good communication:* A leader has to convey his or her expectations to his or her team so that the team can work as per those expectations and deliver results accordingly. A leader has to understand his or her team's expectations and challenges as well so that the same can be addressed and the team delivery could not suffer due to that. Besides that, a leader has to make his or her team understand the vision, mission, values, policies and processes of the organization so that the team can work and behave accordingly while at work. If the leader is not having good communication skills, then he or she will not be able to do these activities properly and in that case his or her team will not be delivering expected results and will not be behaving as per organization's expectations. This will further result into an unsuccessful team. So, communication is one of the core skills of a leader and a leader must be sharpening it all the time during his or her entire career. When we say communication that does not mean only speaking instead it means speaking plus listening. So, a leader must be a good listener as well as a good speaker. Listening is not hearing, a leader needs to be an active listener that means he or she needs to pay full attention while listening, write important points that is being listened, ask short questions in between to clarify information and give empathetic expressions as and when needed. All these things will help the leader to understand people's concern in a better way.

A leader needs to be a very good speaker as well. As a speaker a leader always needs to remember "*It is important to put our view points to others but it is more important to take care HOW you are putting that!!!*". It means only right use of words is not important while speaking but how (body language, voice tone, voice modulation etc.) those words are being spoken is also very important. Different body language, voice tone and modulation make a different meaning all together when used with the same words. So as a speaker we need to pay good attention to them (body language, voice tone and modulation). Besides this a speaker always needs to be audience centric that means he or she always tries to convey the information in a way that audience wants to understand, not the information that he or she as speaker wants to say. A good speaker always assesses the interest area, knowledge level, cultural and religious preferences etc. of his or her audience and then keeps his or her words, body language and voice tone and modulation accordingly so that the audience can understand the message in a right way.

Besides listening and speaking, a leader has to use two more forms of communication very often. They are writing and presenting. While writing the leader needs to be remember "We should write to convey the intended messages only but not to show case our language knowledge level". That means we should keep our words simple so that anyone and everyone can understand it. We should keep our paragraph or entire written communication concise so that people don't need to take out a separate time slot to read our written communication. Along with simple words and concise content, we must need to make sure that our written communication is complete enough to convey the message that we intend to convey.

A leader needs to be a very good presenter as well. A good presenter is the one who manages to make his or her audience understand the message that he or she as a presenter wants to convey. As a presenter the leader should first assesses his or her audience properly in advance and then needs to keep message content, medium of content delivery, body language and voice tone and modulation accordingly so that audience can understand the message with the same meaning that presenter wants to convey. Steve jobs, founder of Apple Inc. was one of the best presenter of the world. To convey the message "This is the thinnest laptop of the world" he used to keep the laptop in an envelope while giving presentation. To convey the message on the storage size of an Apple mobile phone, he did not use giga byte as unit to convey the storage capacity instead he used to say, "This phone can store 7000 songs". He was doing this so that technical, semi technical as well as non-technical audience can understand his message.

So, if you want to become a successful leader in future then you will have to develop a very good communication skill that includes listening, speaking, writing and presenting. Development on all these skills is a time taking process but if it is done consistently then a person can be a matured communicator after a year or two.

Below are few suggestions from me to improve your communication skill:

1- Try having all your professional communication in English. As the entire world now is a global market place so you might need to work in any country at any point of time or with people of any country at any point of time. In that case English is the only connecting language for you two so you must be extremely good at it.

2- Think in English most of the time. In non-English speaking countries people get very less opportunities to communicate in English. So, to improve English communication people from such countries can think in English most of the time. This will help them a lot in keeping their speaking and writing fluency good.

3- Read any good English newspaper or magazine at least 30 minutes daily.

4- Watch any good English news channel or movie channel at least 30 minutes daily.

5- Watch interview of any celebrity, famous business tycoon, politician etc. on TV or on internet. Do it at least twice in a month and try to imitate the body language, words selection and way of speaking.

6- Watch any new product or service release presentation on TV or internet. Do it at least once in a month and try to imitate the way presentation is given.

As an inspiring leader, please do all these 6 things for a year or two and I guarantee that your communication skills will be impressive enough to help you succeed as a leader.

❖ ***Balanced Mindset:*** Under any circumstances a leader needs to maintain a balanced mindset so that he or she cannot lose focus from actual goals.

When I say any circumstances then I really mean any bad or worst circumstances or any good or excellent circumstances. A leader has to face situations very often when something is totally out of the scope of the planning, an employee has committed a mistake that is totally against the processes or policies of the company, a tough customer has made an escalation threatening giving up services or products etc. Under any of these kinds of situations a leader should maintain a balanced mindset so that he or she could not lose focus from the actual objectives. This is very well needed because if leaders get very angry or disappointed or depressed then he or she will not be able to give right guidance to his or her team to handle the situation. So, a leader should maintain a balanced mindset in such situations and give guidance to his or her team to handle the situation in the best possible ways. Sometimes something goes very well unexpectedly in leader's team or organization, in that kind of situation as well a leader should maintain a balanced mindset without getting too excited or extra ordinarily happy so that the leader could not lose focus from actual goals. This is also important to be taken care because we do not lose focus in bad times only, we lose focus from our goals in our good times as well.

Below are few of my suggestions to maintain a balanced mindset as a leader:

1- Please follow my rule of 100% presence. As per this rule you need to be 100% present physically and mentally wherever you are. If you are at your home, be fully present there mentally and physically. Forget all your office affairs completely. When you are at office, be 100% present there physically and mentally. Here also forget all your home affairs completely. This way you will be in a position to take care of your office and home responsibilities in a timely manner and you will be a happy person in both of your worlds. This will help you a lot to have balanced mindset always in life.

2- Work in a problem and solution mode. A leader should always work in problem and solution mode. It means if there is a problem, there must be a solution if you try to find it with a balanced mindset. So as a leader if there is a problem due to a person or situation then never ever get angry, disappointed or depressed of the problem instead immediately assess the problem properly and start looking for solution. In such problematic situations the leader should lead his or her team by giving all possible guidance and support. As a leader you should have a mindset that whatever has happened cannot be stopped going back into the past, but it can be corrected or mitigated, and significant actions can be taken to stop its reoccurrences in future.

3- Be a good risk identifier. A leader needs to be a good risk identifier. In free time a leader needs to focus on all aspects of his or her team or organization and try to find out all possible risks that can hamper the function of the team or the organization. Once a risk is identified, the leader should drive it till the time it is not removed or mitigated at least.

4- Be a good root cause analyser. One thing is sure that the problem already occurred cannot be stopped going back into the past, but it can be stopped from reoccurring in future. That's why a leader must be a good root cause analyser and try to find out the root cause of a problem. Once the root cause is found, the leader must drive it till the time it is either resolved or there are significant things in place to mitigate the impact in future if the same problem reoccurs. One simple technique to do root cause analysis is to ask "Why" 5 times against a problem statement and answer to the 5th "Why" will be the root cause. This is called "5 why root cause analysis". If we analyse a problem statement of a customer escalation, then it will go like this:

1st Why – Why customer escalated?
Answer – Delay in shipment

2nd Why– Why shipment was delayed?
Answer – Order was not processed in time.

3rd Why – Why order was not processed in time?
Answer – Order processing system was down.

4th Why – Why order processing system was down?
Answer – Hardware failure

5th Why – Why there was hardware failure?
Answer – Due to low capacity and too much load

Here the answer to the 5th why is the root cause of the problem so it should be taken care of in order to stop the reoccurrence of the problem in future.

5- Never take anything personally and always go by principles and policies during tough discussions.

Sometimes a leader has to be involved in tough discussions with employees, stakeholders and customers of the organization. In such situations the leader should not take anything personally and should try having discussions as per the policies and principles of the organization. If the other parties are getting out of the way of the professionalism, then the leader should bring them on right track by decently reminding them of the organization principles and policies. This way the leader will be in a position to handle any kind of tough discussions peacefully and professionally.

So, if anyone wants to become a leader in his or her future role then he or she should practice all above suggested things to develop a balanced mindset as part of his or her personality. As a future leader When you will practice these things in your current role then your colleagues and your leaders will notice a change your way of working and they will start taking you as an ideal person or professional. This way your objective of moving towards a leadership role will have some progress. But keep in mind that having a balanced mindset under any situation is one of the main expectations from a leader, so you must develop it as part of your personality.

Before we start the second mantra, lets summarize what we discussed so far as part of our first mantra. First mantra is first be the one that you want to make others. That means every leader wants his or her subordinates or followers to be an ideal person or professional, but it is possible only if the leader himself or herself is ideal. That's why if you want to be a leader in your future role then you will have to be an ideal person and professional in your current role. You will have to follow all the techniques that have been suggested above to become an ideal person and professional. If you comply this mantra successfully in your life, then your leadership journey will begin, and you will be a leader in future for sure.

2nd *Mantra* ───────────────

"Leadership is a lifetime purpose and actions driven mindset, not a designation"

There is a great misconception regarding the definition of leadership. Many people understand leadership as designation, position, power, authority etc. but leadership is none of them. It is a mindset with a life time purpose and a set of actions to meet that purpose. Whosoever is having a purpose to do something innovative, creative, meaningful and value adding to our society, organization, country or the world and is executing a set of actions properly and successfully to meet the purpose, is a leader. First, one has to start executing all those actions successfully as an individual contributor for some time then people start accepting that person a leader by becoming his or her followers. This way the journey of a new leader starts and the process of executing leadership relevant actions and getting acceptance from followers; goes on for a year or two or even more depending on situation then the new leader is given a leadership designation, position, power and authority. If a person becomes a leader in this way, then his or her success probability as a leader is very high because as a leader he or she is quite good at the execution of all leadership related actions and he or she has already earned the acceptance of his or her followers. So, the leader is not only a designated leader but he or she is an accepted leader as well. On the contrary if someone is designated as a leader directly by existing senior leaders then the person may not be good at the execution of leadership related actions and he or she may not get acceptance of his or her would be followers. People gets attracted towards a leader looking at his or her leadership related actions execution capability and their success rate. But in this case the new leader has not executed any leadership related actions at all so if he or she starts executing now then there are high chances of some failures. Such failures will not throw good impressions on the followers and they will further get distracted from their newly designated leader. This way the success probability of such a leader is very low.

One thing we all need to understand very clearly that leader should be accepted as a leader by his or her followers or subordinates. If the leader is not accepted as a leader by his or her people then person is a not a leader but a leadership designation, position or title holder. Such unaccepted leadership designation holder never gets successful in the leadership mission.

Leadership is a life time mindset under which a person understands a bigger purpose of his or her life, sets future vision/s accordingly and execute all things needed to get the purpose fulfilled. No formal designation or position or title is needed to have this kind of mindset and to proceed further accordingly. If you want to be a leader then you will have to develop such a mindset so that you can see a bigger purpose of your life and set future visions with execution strategies accordingly. Once your visions and execution strategies are ready then you will have to execute them at full of your capacity. This way your visions will be realized one after another and finally your end purpose will be fulfilled.

When Mahatma Gandhi was thrown out of the first class reserved compartment of a train as Indians were not allowed in first class reserved compartments those days, he thought a lot over that incident and got a life time leadership mindset with a purpose to make India free from British rule. In order to fulfil his purpose, he had many visions and made many execution strategies. He executed them all one by one in the forms of various movements and kept getting his various visions realized one by one. At the end on 15th August 1947 his end purpose of free India was fulfilled. This is just to remind you that when Mahatma Gandhi started his journey to make India free, he was not having any formal leadership designation or position, but he kept doing all the actions that a leader should do and later he was designated as the father of the nation in India.

So, to be a leader in future, you will have to have a leadership mindset first to find a big purpose of your life. Then you will have to set many visions and strategies to be executed to get that big purpose fulfilled. When you will travel half way on this kind of leadership journey then a formal leadership designation, position, authority and title will come to you. But to become a leader you will have to start your journey without these formal entitlements. To become a leader mastery at the execution of below set of leadership actions is needed; not a designation. Once you are doing excellent on the execution of all the below set of actions, the leadership title or designation will come to you on its own. You should align all these actions with the big purpose of your life and execute them at full capacity of yours.

❖ *Understand expectations out of you & Deliver more than 100%:* To be a leader in your future role you will have to deliver excellent results against your current role expectations. In order to do so you will have to follow the suggestions given under high performance as part of the first mantra. Your only objective here is to become an ideal person and professional. you will have to be a high performer to be accepted as an ideal person and professional by your colleagues and by your existing leaders.

To deliver more than 100%, first of all understand the vision, mission and values of your organization by your self-efforts and with the help of your manager or HR. Then with the help of your manager understand your personal goals as well as the goals of your department. Once you fully understand all these things then align your way of working and behaviour as per your organization vision, mission, values, your personal goals and your department goals. Here you will have to use your full physical, mental and intellectual capacity to deliver against your goals then only you will be able to deliver more than 100%.

Few tips I would like to give here to help you to be a high performer:

1- Prepare a daily to do list every day in the beginning of your work start hours. This list should have the action items you have to finish today and make sure you are finishing them that day only. But in case you are not finishing them then make sure you finish the pending one the very next day on priority.

2- Maintain an action item tracker for the actions that are time taking and you have to complete. Review it twice in a week and push all action items at your level best.

3- Do proper time management. First complete your required work then only go for coffee or refreshment break with your friends. Never postpone your work for the last hours of the day. Come office at time, finish all your required work in time and leave office in time. You can also follow my rule of 100% presence to better manage your time.

4- Never hesitate to ask for help or guidance from your senior colleagues and manager. If you feel the need of it, then ask for it as soon as possible.

5- Keep your manager updated on monthly basis for the progress made on the action items you are working on and also ask for his feedbacks or suggestions. You can do this by having a face to face discussion for 15-20 minutes or you can also write an email for the same. It will be very well if you do both. First drop an email then have a quick discussion for 15-20 minutes to brief your manager for the content of the email.

❖ *Always Keep yourself fully updated:* Keep yourself fully updated about the things happening in your department and organization. This is needed so that you as an aspiring leader, can adjust your way of working and behaviour accordingly. This will help you a lot in becoming an ideal person and professional in your organization. I would like to remind you again that you will have to become an ideal person and professional first before becoming a leader. Moreover, you will have to be accepted as an ideal person and professional by your colleagues and existing leaders then only progress towards your future leadership role will have a movement.

Being fully updated of the things happening in environment in which an organization is operating; is one of the main quality of a leader. A leader needs to do it so that he or she can plan or change his or her way of planning or working accordingly. This is very important for the success of the organization and even for personal success. That's why as a would-be leader you will have to very good at this habit.

I would give below suggestions to help you doing this:

1- Visit your organization intranet portal on daily basis. Now a days all organizations have such portal that is used to share information with employees. So, visit that on daily basis and spend 20-30 minutes of time there looking for and reading the new information that has been posted. There will be many days when you will not find anything new so just close the portal and procced with you other work. But please visit such portal of your organization on daily basis.

2- Visit your organization public website once in a month and go over the new information that you find there. Spend 30-40 minutes of your time there in a month to do it. This will give you lots of information like what are the new things your organization is doing, what technology they are bringing in etc. All such information will be very important for you to leverage your ongoing mission that is to become a leader.

3- Read all top leadership or HR mails completely and by spending some time on them. Sometimes organization top leadership sends mail to inform all employees of an organization but most of the employees do not read those emails reason being those mails are usually long. But those mails are having very important information about the organization so as an aspiring leader you must read them properly. This will help you a lot in keeping yourself fully updated about your organization.

4- Participate in meetings like town hall meeting, all employees meeting with top leadership, cross functional team meetings etc. To keep yourself fully updated you must participate in such meetings because they are good source of information and will be very helpful to an aspiring leader like you.

5- Try keeping yourself updated with the information relevant to overall business domain in which your organization is operating. If your organization is doing business in telecommunication domain and then you as an aspiring leader, should keep yourself updated what's going on in the world of telecommunication. You should visit websites of some business forecasting organizations to do so. You should spend 30-60 minutes of time in a month to visit such sites and to go over relevant information.

Please do all the above things in timely manner consistently and keep yourself fully updated with the latest information. Also keep your way of working fully aligned with the ongoing changes in your organization or the entire business domain.

❖ *Initiative, ownership and accountability:* These are 3 golden words of leadership and every leader should be excellent at its execution. A leader should take initiatives to enhance existing things, make a situation better, bring change in people's life and to bring a new thing in place altogether. After taking an initiative, a leader should own it till completion. Ownership means monitoring, measuring, guiding and pushing forward every aspect of all the activities that are in execution to complete the new initiative in expected time. At the end when the initiative is completed, a leader should hold only himself or herself accountable for the end results if results are negative. But if end results are positive then a leader should give the entire success credit to his or her team. It sounds weird that failure should be taken up by a leader, but the success should be given to the team but that's what rule of successful leadership is and there is a very sound rationale behind this rule. When an initiative fails, lots of finger pointing activities start with questions like who did it, why it happened, what were the mistakes, who should be held accountable for this failure etc. All these questions are correct in a situation when something had failed, and their answers will give good input to stop reoccurrences of similar failures in future. But if answers to such questions are searched in finger pointing mode then found answers will be incorrect because everybody involved will try to save himself or herself by manipulating the facts. In such a situation the leader can dig down up to certain limit to do fact findings but he or she will not be able to find the actual facts because the supplier of the facts are the involved parties in the failure and they will never present raw facts. On the contrary if the leader holds himself or herself accountable for the failure then answer to all above questions will be facts. Let me explain you how it should be handled by the leader. Whenever anything fails in an organization, the leader should immediately accept the accountability for the same. At the same time, he or she should express his or her trust in his or her team by conveying a message in person verbally if possible or by sending a mail. Here the leader should convey very clearly that his or her team is a group of fantastic people and the same team will try for the same initiative once again but with a different way of working. Such a message from the leader will remove fear from the minds of the team and they will believe that they are not going to be the scapegoat for the failure. Now they will provide facts against all those questions that are usually searched for during root cause analysis of such failures. The leader should take full advantage of the situation and should have complete root cause analysis done. At the end if leader comes to know that the failure is due to any person or people mistakes then the leader should not punish that person or those people because today they made a mistake but tomorrow they may do wonderful jobs if their mistakes are corrected by right mentorship and facilitation. On the contrary if people who made mistakes are punished then rest of the people will be scared of trying something new or doing a job with creativity. In such a situation, growth of organization will not be possible because employees would not like to do anything different or anything new or anything challenging as they will be scared of mistakes and subsequent punishments. So instead of punishing people for the failure, the leader should try to correct the reasons for the mistakes be it people mistakes, process mistakes or technology mistakes. When such corrections will be done then reoccurrences of similar failures will be stopped, and team morale will also be preserved. That's what the job of a leader is to stop repeated failures and to keep employee's morale high. This way just by accepting the accountability for a failure the leader justifies his or her role successfully.

At the same time the leader must remember that making mistakes is not bad but making similar mistakes repeatedly is bad for the organization that's why person or people responsible for repeated mistakes must be handled as per organization employee's performance management policies.

Whenever any initiative of a leader is successful then the leader should give its entire credit to his or her team because success of a leader is measured by the success of his or her team. But when the leader gives such credit to his or her team, the morale of the team goes many folds high and the team pushes themselves for something far bigger and gets loyal to the leader and the organization. That's why a leader should accept the accountability of a failure and give success credit to his or her team.

Sometimes a leader might have to face some criticism, tough questions and even warnings from some stakeholders of the organization in case failure and acceptance of accountability. The leader enjoys more positional and authoritative power in the organization than his or her team members so he or she will be able to manage all those things in a tactful manner. But if the team members are made accountable for the failures then they will not be able to manage all those tough things and resulting situation will not be good for anyone; be it team members, organization and even the leader. As the team members will be getting lose confidence at work, organization will get a low morale employee and the leader will get a team that is low at confidence and morale. That's why it is the responsibility of the leader to lead to his or her team from the front in case of failure.

You can use 3 golden words of leadership in your personal life as well. Take initiatives to make things better in your life, drive that initiative with a sense of ownership till completion and be self-accountable for the end results. Hold yourself accountable in case of failure or success. Usually people hold themselves accountable in case of success but in case of failure they start blaming others or a situation or thing. This is not correct because unless you accept accountability for your failure, you will not be taking lessons out of it. So, one should hold himself or herself accountable for one's failure and should do proper root cause analysis of the failure to take lessons out of it and to put preventive measures in place so that similar failures could not occur again.

To be a leader in your future role, you should start using these 3 golden words of leadership in your personal as well as professional life. The main problem with many individual contributors is that they don't know how to take initiatives and take things further that's why below are some of my key suggestions to them:

1- In your free time, think over the various aspects of your personal and professional life and prepare a list of items that can be improved further remarkably. Also think of value adding new things that can be put into place and update such things in your list as well. Once your list has at least 5 items then assign priority against each of them like high, medium and low.

2- In next 2-3 days, take out at least one hour of time from your schedule and think over possible solution as an improvement or as a new thing altogether for each of the item of your list. To find solution do some research on internet and consolidate your findings in a presentable document be it Microsoft excel or PowerPoint. Make sure your document is having justification for why the new thing or change is needed, how it will be implemented, what will be the benefits etc.

3- Share that presentable document with your manager over mail and ask for his or her time to discuss the same.

4- During your discussion, convince your manager for your initiatives with your justifications.

5- Your manager may disagree with few of your initiatives and he will explain you the reason for the same. On such occasion you don't need to get discouraged instead you need to proceed with the initiatives that you manager agrees to and approves to proceed further. During this meeting if you feel the need of taking some other colleague help then ask your manager to allocate that resource to work with you. Be a good team player while working on your initiatives.

Now as you have understood the importance of the 3 golden words of leadership so start practising them as an individual contributor as per the above suggestions so that you can be taken as an ideal person and professional by your colleagues and manager. Besides that, you will be in a habit of taking initiatives to make things better. Your this habit will help you a lot when you will be in a leadership role.

❖ *Be a team player:* A leader has to be a great team player. Whatever the leader does, he or she should take his or her team together because success of the leader is defined by the success of his or her team. I have already explained the meaning and purpose of team work in team work section of my first mantra so please refer it once again and try to make your entire team successful by practising the things suggested there.

As you are an individual contributor now and want to be a leader in your future role, so you will have to develop team work as one of your core competency because you will never become a leader without this competency and even if you become by luck then you will never be successful as a leader without this competency. Most of the individual contributors do not practise team work because they are scared of getting their own competitors being helped directly or indirectly. They think if they become a team player then their fellow colleagues will be benefited in terms of knowledge, competency, exposure etc. and very soon they (individual contributor's colleagues) will rise like theirs (individual contributors) competitors. I would like to make one thing very clear based on my own experience that whenever you extend help to anyone in raising his or her knowledge, competency, exposure etc. then your own grows many folds. At the same time, you are accepted as an ideal person and professional by your colleagues and leaders. Below are some suggestions for you:

1- Surrender the feeling of "I will win" and arouse the feeling of "We will win".

2- Help your colleagues by sharing your knowledge. At least once in a month organize a knowledge sharing session with your colleagues and impart knowledge on a topic that you are good at and is relevant to your work domain.

3- Extend help to your colleagues in execution of complex action items. If any of your colleague is stuck in a complex task, then extend your assistance on your own and help him or her out.

4- Extend help to your colleagues by sharing their workload. If any of your colleague is having lots of work load and you have some free time then extend some assistance.

5- Invite your colleagues to join your initiatives and extend your participation in their initiatives as well. Whenever you take an initiative then invite few of your worthy colleagues to be part of your execution group similarly if any of your colleague takes an initiative then extend your participation on your own.

Please practise all these above things as an individual contributor so that you can have team work as one of your professional competency.

❖ *Motivate your colleagues:* A leader should be a great motivator. In adverse time people expect their leader to uplift their morale so that they can be ready to face the situation and come out of that successfully. This is also one of the core competency of a leader and it takes time to acquire. To be able to motivate others, the leader first needs to be a self-motivated person and to be a self-motivated person, one has to read and watch lots of motivational contents and also needs to practise the same by trying to motivate others. It's a time taking process but if it goes on for a year or so then the person becomes very good self-motivated person and a motivator for others as well. Every leader should try their best to acquire the capability of motivating others because this is a game changing capability. There are many examples in sports, business, politics and warfare that a team or a company or a party or an army unit was about the lose game or the business or political power or the war but in the very last moment the leader motivated his or her people so well that they changed scenario completely. As we all know that Steve Jobs founded a Company called Apple and he grew that company significantly in next few years. When company became big many new people also joined that and many outsiders also invested in the company and few of the big investors became company board members. Everything was going well but Steve Jobs brought a CEO to manage the company so that he can also learn management practices from him over a period of time as he (Steve Jobs) was from a technical background and was not good at management in those early days of his career. Initial few months went well for the new CEO and Steve Jobs but later both started having differences of opinion that kept growing. At one occasion the new CEO wanted Steve Jobs to focus on management and governance side of company only but Steve Jobs was heavily involved in product design and engineering division of the company and he was not ready to leave that at any cost. Because for him (Steve Jobs) the main goal of his company was to give quite a unique product to customers. Both could not sort out this difference and the matter reached the company board for resolution. In board meeting, most of the board members took side of the new CEO and Steve Jobs was asked to leave the company he had founded. After leaving Apple Steve Jobs founded 2 more companies and did many innovative things there as well. On the other hand, Apple performance kept degrading day by day. Many CEOs were changed but no one could stabilize the company. Almost after a decade when Apple was on the verge of collapse then few members of the company board decided to bring Steve Jobs back to stabilize the company. Steve Jobs was first given a position in the board of Apple and later he became CEO of the company. When he took position in Apple board he realized that the morale the good employees of the company was low due to poor performance of the company. So, he addressed employees and said that still there were employees in the company who were doing great jobs but due to the poor and irrelevant strategies of the company they were doing great jobs on things that are irrelevant to Apple. This statement made good impact on the employee's morale. Then Steve Jobs changed the strategies of the company and took Apple to its new height once again.

I would like to give the example of Jack Ma also. Today Jack Ma is one of top richest people of China but when he founded his company Alibaba, his business was not good initially for 2 – 3 years. That time most of his employees were having partnership in the company. Though revenue of the company was not coming as expected but Jack Ma was getting lots of emails from his customers that they were liking his services and they believed that his service would make them successful. This kept Jack Ma motivated all the time during those tough days. In every employee meeting Jack Ma was telling his employees that they were not from a family of businessmen, they did not have a rich father or a powerful uncle so if they became successful, they would create history for the next generation. This statement used to motivate his employees a lot and most of them worked with him for a long time. After few years company started doing good business and became one of the well-known company of the world.

As a would-be leader, you will have to develop this competency in yourself while being in your current role only because it takes time to build and by the time you will be a leader in future, you will be a very good self-motivated person and a great people motivator.

Below are some of my suggestions to help you on this:

1- Watch at least one or two motivational videos daily on youtube.com.
2- Read at least one or two motivational books in a year. I recommend you to read all books written on the life of Steve Jobs and Jack Ma.
3- Whatever you learn out of your above 2 actions, bring it in use in your life.
4- Motivate your colleagues using the positive things happening in your department or organization.
5- You can also use some publicly available motivational content on internet to motivate your colleagues.

If you start doing all these things as an individual contributor, then right after a year you will be a very good self-motivated person and a great people motivator.

❖ *Disconnect Yourself from Negative Talks:* Nothing is perfect in this world be it a person, place, thing or an organization. There is always a scope of improvement for everything and people related are supposed to work on that improvement area to take that person, place, thing or an organization towards perfection. But there are people in our society or organization who can only talk negative about areas where improvements are needed but they will never do anything to bring improvement in those areas. In every society or organization, you will find such people. They will exaggerate any issue in such a way that it could never be solved. As a would-be leader you should stay away from such people but if you come across them at any time and you hear any such gossip then you should softly disconnect yourself from on-going negative talks about your department or organization. If you come across such gossips very often then only you should inform your next level manager so that he or she can handle the situation accordingly. Because such gossips spread negativity in the team or in the organization that impacts the morale and way of working of the employees. You should never try to fix such situation on your own because people responsible for such gossips will never listen to you and an argument may break out as well. In either case your relationship with your those colleagues will be strained. Such strained relationship with colleagues will not be good for you as an aspiring leader because to be a leader in future you should be accepted by most of your colleagues as an ideal person and professional.

As an ideal person and professional, we should not make areas of improvement as points of negative gossip, instead we should highlight such areas to our next level manager, HR or even top leadership people as and when we get opportunity. Now a day's top leadership of organization also interacts with employees via town hall address, all hands meetings etc. Such occasions can be used to highlight such issues but first such issues should be raised to the next level manager and the local HR.

We should also take initiatives against all such improvement areas and should reach next level manager and local HR with some suggestions as solutions. All such efforts will solve those things in an organization so, we should do it seriously as and when needed.

❖ *Inter Team and Intra Team Communication:* Communication is key to success. If you want to be successful in your personal and professional life, then you will have to communicate with people. When you communicate with others then you come to know their strengths, weaknesses, likes, dislikes, aspirations, choices etc. and vice versa. Such information helps you find out the opportunities you can create for others or others can create for you. You also come to know what value you can add in their lives and they understands what values they can add in your life. This way both parties get opportunities for each other. I call it opportunities because no value addition is done for free there are always some associated benefits. So as a leader or as a would-be leader you should maintain very good level of communication within your team and with other teams of your organization so that you can come to know of some opportunities that is beneficial for all. Maintaining very good level of inter team and intra team communication is again one of the core quality of a leader and as an aspiring leader you should develop it in yourself at your level best. By maintaining communication, I mean creating a platform for such communication, opening various channels for such communication and encouraging people to have such communication.

Below are some suggestions to help you develop and manage such communications:

1- Spend some time during your lunch break or tea/ coffee break with different people of your team and other teams. You should not confine yourself with a fixed group of people only. This is the most common mistake people commit, they spend such times with the fixed limited group of people they know.

2- Pick up few topics from your work domain and propose some knowledge sharing sessions to your team colleagues and to the people from other teams also. Before proposing this to people, take the approval for the same from you manager.

3- Encourage people from your team and from other teams as well, to take similar kind of knowledge sharing session.

4- Encourage people from your team and from other teams as well, to take some common initiatives and work together to benefit all and the overall organization.

5- On occasion of any festival or special days, propose some cross functional activities to your manager and local HR and convince them to approve the same. After getting approval, play a very active role in organizing the same.

As an aspiring leader if you do such kind of things then your inter team and intra team communication will be very good. This will help you a lot in getting many opportunities for your future success. Moreover, you will acquire competency at maintaining communication across organization. This competency is needed throughout your career and will be very crucial in your success as a leader.

❖ *Maintain good relationship with all colleagues:* In a team or organization there are people from different geographical locations, religion, caste, community, family background, belief system etc. They all join an organization and a team with a common purpose that is to work for the development of the organization and for self-development as well. That's why it is the professional responsibility of each employee of the organization that every person should work with each other despite above said differences. Instead each should respect each other nationality, religion, caste, community, belief system etc. and should maintain good professional relationship with each other so that all can work together like one team and can do their best for the end objective of the team or the organization. To be a leader in your future role you will have to be quite good at building good professional relationship in such a diverse organizational culture because you should be accepted in your team as an ideal person and professional. Even after becoming a leader, you will have to manage such a diverse team of people so it's better for you to start developing relationship building skills now so that by the time you become a leader, you will be a matured professional for this skill. That time you will have to use this skill a lot as you will have to manage such a team and to produce expected results, you will have to take everyone together.

Below are some of my suggestions to help you on this:

1- Whenever you start your work, right in the beginning spend 5-10 minutes of time in exchanging greetings with your work place nearby colleagues.

2- Maintain birth day list of your team colleagues and send them wishes on mail. Also wish them in person whenever they meet in office.

3- Do not confine yourself to a group while taking lunch break or coffee break. Keep changing your group after every 2-3 weeks. This way you will be familiar with all your colleagues and will get chance to build good professional relationship with all.

4- While having a general discussion on politics, sports, movies, culture, religion etc., be very careful before you make any comment so that you cannot offend the feelings or beliefs of others.

5- Extend support to all the colleagues who are in need. If someone is having lots of work load or handling a complex work etc. then extend your help before they ask for it.

Please follow all these things as an aspiring leader to build and maintain good professional relationship with your colleagues. If you want to be a successful leader in your future role then you will have to be Master of Building and maintain good professional relationship.

❖ *Have Balanced and Controlled Mindset:* This is one of the main quality of a leader. A leader should always have a balanced and controlled mindset so that he or she cannot lose focus from the actual goals. I have already mentioned it quite in detail under balanced mindset section of my first mantra so please refer that section again and practice all suggested things to have a mindset like this.

Before we move to the third mantra, I would like to conclude my second mantra knowledge here. As per my second mantra leadership is not a designation instead it is a life time purpose and actions driven mindset. So, to be a leader in future, you will have to start doing all the actions that are suggested above. If you do it successfully then formal designation of the leadership will travel to you on its own. So, start your leadership journey with these above set of actions execution to have leadership formal designation and authority in future.

3rd *Mantra* ————————————

"Offload some of your boss workload on your shoulders"

There is a belief in the professional world that people should not promoted unless they are ready for their next job level roles. This means at the current job level only enable a person for more than 50% of the things, he or she will be dealing with at his or her next level job and once the person is ready then only promote him or her to the next job level. This kind of promotion ensures high chances of success at the next level job. There are many multi-national companies where promotions are done by this process only. At least a year before than actual promotion, few prospects employees are chosen based on their current performance, for their next job level promotion and for next one year they are trained, guided, mentored and given assignments relevant to their next job level. After a year if their performance is found to be satisfactory then only they are promoted to their next job level. So, if you want to be promoted to a leadership role in future then you will have to enable yourself first for that promotion by getting yourself ready for more than 50% of leadership competencies so that you can easily manage your responsibilities once you will be given readership role. That's why my third mantra is advising you to offload some of your boss workload on your shoulders. When you assist your boss in his or her work then you get best opportunities to learn your boss work and that's what this third mantra is suggesting you to do.

It will not be an easy task, but it can be done by executing the below action items seriously:

❖ *Prepare a list of self - doable action items out of your boss responsibilities and get it delegated to yourself:* Approximately 20 – 30% of your boss action items are fully streamlined and can be done any SMART person. By smart person I mean, the person who is having reasonably good common sense, good communication skills, decency and passion to excel in life. Such action items are usually a periodic report that your boss sends, a periodic meeting that your boss attends, a special task that only your boss completes in your team because only he or she has the access for the same etc. All I want to say is that every manager has few such action items that can be delegated to another person without any issues. So, prepare list of such few action items of your boss and organize them in a presentable document like Microsoft excel or PowerPoint. In your presentable document mention what that action item is, what your manager does and why you think it can be delegated to you. Once your presentable document is ready then send it to your boss over mail and ask for his or her time for a discussion over it. During your face to face discussion with your boss, try your best to convince him or her to delegate those action items to you. Your boss will definitely ask you the reason to have such delegation. As an answer you can tell him or her that your first objective is to learn from him or her as your future career roadmap is towards leadership role. At the same time, you can also tell him or her that you also want to offload some burden from his or her (your boss) shoulders so that he or she can focus on some new or more challenging activities. Your boss may approve the delegation of some of the action items and for some he or she may not, so you should not worry about that. Instead you should ask your boss to train you on the ones that he or she is ready to delegate you. Once delegated to you, do your best and execute the delegated action item without any error. This way you will offload some work load from your boss and you will get opportunities to learn things for your next job level. So, you will be enabling yourself for your next job level. Keep doing this act of proposing delegation and getting it delegated; repeatedly at certain time interval at least twice in a year.

❖ *Learn 50 – 60 % of your boss work:* A smart person can easily learn 50-60% of his or her boss work while being at current job level only. This can be done by doing two things:

1- By getting your boss streamlined action items delegated to yourself as suggested above.
2- By learning your boss publicly visible action items on self-support basis.

I have already explained point one quite in detail as above that's why I will explain only point two here. There will be many action items that your boss would not like to delegate to you. Reason for the same can be your organization policy or interest of your boss. But you will have to learn those things as you have to enable yourself for your next job level that is a leadership role. Examples of such action items are addressing team meeting, giving performance feedback to employees, presenting your team or department status report to higher management, taking interviews etc. Knowing all such action items is very important for your development as a future leader so please follow my below suggestions:

1- Prepare a list of action items that your boss is not ready to delegate to you or can't delegate to you due to your organization policy. Such action items are publicly visible so preparing a list will not be a tough task.

2- Assign priority like high, medium, low to each of the action item as per their importance in your future leadership role. Now you have to learn all these action items in order of their priority.

3- Search and download relevant videos from youtube.com and watch them couple of times.

4- Search and buy relevant books on Amazon or any other E-commerce site and read them couple of times.

5- Practice and rehearse whatever you learn by your above efforts. You can get opportunity to practice some of the things you learnt like addressing team meeting. If your boss is not available on a day and that day is scheduled for your team meeting, then you should propose your boss to address the team meeting in his or her behalf. Keep your eyes and ear open looking for such other opportunities and practice your lessons learnt. Still there will be action items that you will not get opportunity to practice in your current role, so you will have to rehearse them at your home. Rehearse at your home that how you would interview a candidate, how you would present your team or department status report, how you would give performance feedbacks to employees etc. when you would be a team leader or manager in your future roles. Such practices and rehearsals will make you confident for action items concerned and after becoming a leader in your future when you would be doing it first time, no one would say that you are doing that first time in your life and you will be doing it in an excellent way.

As a would-be leader you will have to learn 50-60% of your boss works while being at your current role only. Because you will have to first enable yourself for your promotion to a leadership role then only you will be promoted to that role in future. So please follow the above suggested things to enable yourself for your future leadership role.

❖ *Create a Virtual Team to assist you:* If you are feeling burdened after getting few delegations then feel free to involve other likeminded junior colleague of yours. This can be a situation as you will have to manage your own routine works as well as your boss delegated works. If you face such a situation then speak to your likeminded junior colleagues and convince them to join you in that journey as they will get unique experience out of it and such experience will be very good for their future career. That is the fact whosoever will be part of this journey, will be benefitted in his or her future career. Once few of your such colleagues are ready then inform your boss about those colleagues and convince your boss that those colleagues will assist you doing the delegated work and they will be back up resources when you will not be available but for your boss you will be the single point of contact for all delegated action items and you will be accountable for their completion. Your this answer will satisfy your boss and then you can proceed with your journey in a balanced way.

So, how you should work now; you will divide few of delegated action items activities among your junior colleagues and will encourage them to complete them in time. At the same time, you will also pick up some of them and will complete them. Once all action items are complete then only you will hand over them to your boss as you are the only point of contact for your boss. In case of any mistakes you will be accountable for that, so you need to supervise and train your colleagues accordingly. Keep in mind that you should never be bossy or tough to your colleagues for the completion or errors of tasks given because in that case they will stop supporting you facing such behaviour from your side. Instead you can use your motivational techniques and friendly behaviour to take the best out of them. This way you will get a virtual team to assist you in handling your boss delegated action items and you will be in a position to manage both your actual work as well those delegated ones. Besides that, you will be in a position to take more delegations as well.

Before moving forward to the fourth mantra, let's summarize the third mantra. The main purpose of 3rd mantra is to enable you for your next job level promotion by giving you, hands on experience of your next level job and by raising your knowledge level to do your next level job. So, I suggest you to do all above action items to practise this mantra so that you can be set for your next job level promotion.

4ᵗʰ *Mantra* ─────────────

"Read and learn a lot on your own"

A leader is supposed to be the navigator of his or her team in any situation. Navigation in right direction and at right speed is not possible if the leader's knowledge level in the concerned work domain and leadership practices is not appropriate. In today's time everything is changing very fast be it technology, standards, best practices, competition and the business environment overall. All these things are changing continually so a leader needs to be a life time student so that he or she can keep learning new things in timely manner and keep managing his or her team accordingly to achieve the expected goals in such a dynamic world.

As part of my first mantra under supreme knowledge section, I have already mentioned the importance of good knowledge in your development as a leader, so I will recommend you to go over that (supreme knowledge section of 1ˢᵗ mantra) once again. To become a leader or to sustain as a successful leader, you will have to take the responsibility of your knowledge enhancement in your own hands. Many people sit idle and do nothing on their own for their knowledge enhancement because they think that enhancing employee's knowledge is the responsibility of the organization. That's true but organization level employee's knowledge enhancement programmes take time to come into reality as it goes through many bureaucratic processes of evaluation and approvals. So, if you keep sitting idle waiting for such programmes then you will be doing nothing but delaying your own growth. Moreover, organization level training programmes may not be fully relevant to your personal growth plan as it is intended to benefit the entire organization not only you. Here I strongly recommend you to take full responsibility of your knowledge enhancement in your own hands and drive that as per my suggestions given under supreme knowledge section of my first mantra as well as few more suggestions I am mentioning below:

❖ *Know more than Your colleagues:* Always keep a target for yourself that you will always know at least more than double than your counterparts in the same organization or industry. Make sure that you are having this target throughout your life and you are chasing this as well with full capacity of yours. You need to understand it very clearly that to be a leader or to stay like a successful leader you will have to know always more than your colleagues. To manage your target, prepare a knowledge management tracker in Microsoft Excel by having columns like Knowledge area, scope, self-study plan, status and remarks. Fill this tracker with all the knowledge enhancement activities that you want to execute to enhance your knowledge overall. Once this tracker is complete then start executing all these activities in order of their priority. Review this tracker at least once in a week and figure out whether you are making progress as expected or not. In case of insufficient progress in any area, accelerate your efforts accordingly. Try learning most of the things by your self-efforts like watching related videos on youtube.com or other relevant sites, reading relevant books, if knowledge area is related to IT then set up a test lab and do practical activities there, ask your senior colleagues for their mentorship or guidance etc. After some time if you feel like having some external trainings at some training centre then never hesitate to do that. Because today if you invest in your knowledge enhancement then tomorrow it will return many folds in different ways.

❖ ***Better Time management:*** Time management will play a very significant role in your self-knowledge enhancement. Manage your time well and take out at least an hour daily to learn something new and relevant to you. Please don't give excuse to be busy because even the busiest people of the world spend good amount of time on learning new things. Warren Buffett spends 4-5 hours of his time daily in reading books, newspapers, magazines etc. Bill Gates and Mark Zuckerberg reads around 40 – 45 books in a year just grow their knowledge.so just think if these people can take some time out to enhance their knowledge they why we cannot do the same. We all need to make a commitment to ourselves that every morning we will wake up more knowledgeable than the previous day.

   Below are my suggestions to manage your time well so that you can have some time to enhance your knowledge:

1- Start your day by writing your to do list. Make sure you are writing something here for your knowledge enhancement. Also do your best so that all your action items are complete before you go to sleep at night.
2- Follow the rule of 100% presence.

3- Fix your time slots for 15-20 minutes couple of times in a day to address your social media activities and attend these activities at those fixed time only.

4- Go to bed in time and try getting up early by completing 7-8 hours of your sleep so that you can be an early riser and have a long day compared to your colleagues.

5- Take care of your health by paying attention to your food, exercise and other hygiene factors because if you get ill then you will lose lots of time doing nothing productive to grow yourself. You should always remember one thing that to be successful in life you need to have a very successful health so that you can work hard and work more than your competitors.

❖ *Periodic self-review of the progress made:* There is a saying in management "whatever we pay our attention to, shows positive developments". This means if you want to make something to develop then start paying attention to it. So, in order to grow our knowledge, we should monitor its progress against our plans. In case of our knowledge enhancement progress monitoring we should use our knowledge management tracker to monitor the progress. We should set a reminder in our mobile, calendar etc. on weekly reoccurring basis as per our availability so that we can get reminders at that time to get this review done. After getting such reminder we should open the tracker concerned and do a thorough review of the progress. If we find slow progress for anything then we should accelerate our efforts, there to make the progress as per our plan.

Before moving to the 5th and the last mantra, I would like to summarize the 4th mantra. The fourth mantra is all about encouraging you to enhance your knowledge on self-support basis because it is your knowledge enhancement, so it should be your responsibility only to enhance it. So, you should do your best to enhance your knowledge by your self-support activities like self-study, taking guidance and mentorship of your senior colleagues and attending trainings in training institutes. This mantra will lay a great foundation for your success by putting a vast reservoir of knowledge in your personality, so you need to practice it well.

5ᵗʰ *Mantra* ————————————

"Maintain good Work Life balance"

To be truly successful in your life you will have to be successful in your personal and professional life both. Because if you are very successful in your professional life but your personal life is messed up then you will not be able to fully enjoy the privileges of your professional success. Similarly, if you are not successful in your professional life then you will mess up your personal life due to various scarcities. So, maintain a very good balance between your personal and professional life so that you can manage both well and you can be successful in both. If you want to be a leader in future then you will have to be extremely good at maintaining balance between your personal and professional life because it is said that if a person cannot manage the two parts of his or her life (personal and professional) then how that person can manage a business that consists of customers, stakeholders, employees, channel partners, suppliers etc. It's true because if your personal life is not streamlined then you will not be able to focus on your professional life and as a result you will not be able to execute the action items that is important to transform you as a leader from an individual contributor. Thorough execution of all leadership transformation action items requires the best physical, mental and intellectual capabilities of yours as a would-be leader and such best capabilities will never be coming out of you if your personal life is not well settled. So, to become a leader in your future role start settling the issues of your personal life so that you can be in a position to start your preparation for your leadership journey. Once things are in good shape in your personal life then start the execution of all the suggested action items under all the mantras to transform yourself from individual contributor to a leader. Here I am not advising you to make your personal life perfect and free from challenges. Personal life can never be perfect and free from challenges. Always there will be issues like disagreement with spouse on certain things, disobedience issues from children, self and family health issues, financial challenges etc. and as a human being you will have to manage them. But here I am trying to tell you that you should fix the personal life issues that may stop you from executing the action items needed to become a leader. At the same point of time I strongly recommend that while trying to fix anything in your personal life, make sure that your way is always correct from moral, social, spiritual and legal point of view.

Please start executing below action items to have a very good work life balance:

❖ *Discuss your commitment to become a leader with your close family members and ask for their co-operation:* One fine day take your close family members (Parents, spouse, kids, siblings) to a good place for a dinner or lunch. After the lunch or dinner when you return home then request them to sit together for 20-30 minutes and explain them your commitment and further plans to become a leader. During your explanation, let them know why you want to achieve a leadership role, how it will be beneficial for you in future career and how each of them will be benefitted if you achieve your goal successfully. It is true that when you will be successful in your efforts and become a leader then you will be able to extend more support to your family members in terms more privileges, more comfortable life and increased social status. In the end of your discussion you should ask them to extend their best support to help you in this journey. Their support can be in the form of giving top priority to your goal rather a domestic or family work. Unless there is an emergency, this rule of priority should be supported by all family members of yours. Here I am not advising you to rub off your shoulder from all your family responsibilities and focus only on your leadership development. Instead I am trying to tell you that if anything is not urgent or of emergency nature then that should hold second priority in your to do list. But in urgency or emergency situation, you must address the concerned responsibilities of yours as your top priority. By holding second priority of non-urgent or non-emergency things in your to do list, I mean to say that you should focus on doing all your leadership development things first on daily basis then every day you should take some time out to handle such responsibilities of yours in the end. Besides this, delegate some of your family responsibilities to your family members if they can handle on their own without any difficulties. Like your spouse can take your kid or parent for a medical check-up. Your spouse only can attend your kids' teacher parent meeting. Your siblings can manage some of your family work like bringing grocery from a supermarket etc. Try delegating such family responsibilities of yours, if your family members are ready to accept that. I firmly believe that your family members will definitely support you at least on some of things if you ask for their cooperation in this way. But you will have to make best use of such free time in your self-development.

❖ *Follow my "Rule of 100% presence":* To have a very good balanced personal and professional life, I strongly recommend you to follow this rule of mine. I have already mentioned in detail in balanced mindset section of my first mantra so please refer that section once again.

My this rule advises you to be 100% present physically and mentally wherever you are, be it your home or office. This will help you addressing your responsibilities at both the places and you will be a happy person in in both your personal and professional life. Initially you will find it difficult to follow this rule but if you try doing it every day then in a matter of six months your mind will be set to work as per this rule. Once you have this kind of mindset then your success in both lives of yours will be tremendous if you make best use of your physical and mental presence by delivering against your responsibilities at best of your capacity.

❖ *Separate a slice of time for your personal things at your work place:* There are some personal things that we need to address in day time only when we are at work. Examples of such personal works are taking a doctor appointment, speaking to your bank branch office etc. So, to attend such things, we should dedicate a separate time slot and we should always stick to that time slot only to address such things. We should try having such a time slot right after lunch because around that time we don't feel active at work. However, you can choose any time that is suitable for you, but you need to make sure that your time slot is not for more than 30 minutes. During this time slot only, you should give a call to your spouse or kids and you should attend your social media (Facebook, twitter, WhatsApp) activities as well. This way you will be taking care of your personal and professional things even at your work place in a proper manner and you will not mess up one with another as at a time you will be focused on the one only.

❖ *Maintain a "To do list" and an action item tracker:* I have already mentioned this in detail as punctuality section of my first mantra. So please refer to the same again and follow it make your personal and professional life balanced. These two simple tools will help you focus and complete your tasks of personal and professional life in timely manner. This way people at both part of your life will be happy with you. Everyday once you are fresh after getting up in morning, write 2 "to do lists"; one for your personal things and one for your professional things. Then throughout the day chase all items of your "to do lists" and do your best to complete them. Once you complete an item then strike it off using a pen or pencil so that you can remember what you finished and what are still pending for you. At the night before you go to bed have a quick look at your "to do lists" and strike off the ones that are finished and write pending ones to the next day "to do lists" so that you can address them the very next day.

There are issues of your personal and professional life that cannot be finished in one or two days. You should maintain list of such issues in a Microsoft Excel tracker. You should put a reminder in your mobile or calendar to remind you twice in a week to have a look at this tracker so that you can review your progress made and adjust your focus on pending items accordingly. Like we maintained two "to do lists" similarly we need to maintain two action item trackers; one for our personal things and one for our professional things.

❖ *Develop a balanced and controlled mindset:* You need to have very good balanced and controlled mindset to have a well-balanced personal and professional life. I have already explained this quite in details under balanced mindset section of my first mantra. So, you need to revisit that section once again and follow all the practices suggested there. If you follow all the suggested practices with full faith and dedication, then after 6 months your mindset will be balanced and controlled in a situation. This way you will be able to do right thing at right time in your personal and professional life. This action of yours will result into a balanced personal and professional life.

Summary of this Book

This book is designed to help experienced people in individual contributor role to transform themselves into leaders so that they can add more value wherever they are working or whatever they are doing, and they can add more value to their own life as well. It is also designed to help fresh engineering or management graduates to get settled in their professional life soon and start rolling on their growth path from their day one of their professional life.

This book encourages the individual contributor to read the chapter "Have a decisive day in your life" and take a decision whether to become a leader or not. For the people who are committed to become leader, this book recommends five mantras to be followed. Each mantra recommends some action items to be followed to make the above said transformation happen.

The 1st mantra "First be the one that you want to make others", encourages a person to become an ideal first before even thinking of becoming a leader. It suggests many action items to transform a person into an ideal person and professional and also to get him or her accepted as an ideal by his or her colleagues or friends or in his or her social circle.

The 2nd mantra "Leadership is a life time purpose and actions driven mindset, not a designation" advises people to start their leadership journey without a leadership designation. It says that if people are good at the execution of leadership related set of actions then designation will come to them on its own.

The 3rd mantra "Offload some of your boss workload on your shoulders" advises people to become at least 50% ready while being in their current role only for the role they want to be promoted to. It recommends people to start learning the work of their bosses to be ready for their future role.

The 4th mantra "Read and learn a lot on your own" strongly recommends people to enhance knowledge on their own and not be dependent on anyone else to get their knowledge enhanced.

The 5th mantra "Work Life balance" emphasises on maintaining a good balance between our personal and professional life. It suggests many action items to be executed to ensure a good balance between these parts of our life.

Your daily life compliance to five mantras

As you have finished reading this book now so it's time to make the compliance of all the five mantras as part of your daily life. Only knowledge of these mantras is not enough, it will bring positive changes in your life if you practise them on daily basis. Take a Xerox copy of the leadership mantra chart (Available in the next page) and fix it in your bedroom at such a place so that you can see this as a first thing every morning you open your eyes and as the last thing before you sleep. I want you to do this so that you can realize every morning what you have to do to become a leader and every night you can measure yourself whether you are doing enough or not to fulfil your leadership dreams. I suggest you to get up every morning and prepare your daily to do list looking at this chart and make sure that you are having at least one action item for every mantra in your list. This way you will do at least something to transform yourself into a leader. These little steps will get your closure to your goal so please do this as part of your daily life works. Every night before you sleep you should give just five minutes and think over every mantra and take a decision against your progress made for that. If you think, you are doing enough for that then keep it up the way it has been but if you think, you are not doing enough against any of the mantras then you need to take some steps to do that. This way you will be executing, monitoring and enforcing all these five mantras in your life to become a leader soon.

Leadership Mantras Chart

1st **mantra** "First be the one that you want to make others".

Action Items: Passion, Punctuality, Honesty & Integrity, High Performance, Team Work, Supreme Knowledge, Good communication.

2nd **Mantra** "Leadership is a lifetime purpose and actions driven mindset, not a designation".

Action Items: Understand expectations out of you & Deliver more than 100%, Always Keep yourself fully updated, Initiative, ownership and accountability, motivate your colleagues, Disconnect Yourself from Negative Talks, Inter Team and Intra Team Communication, maintain good relationship with all colleagues, Have Balanced and Controlled Mindset.

3rd **Mantra** "Offload some of your boss workload on your shoulders".

Action Items: Prepare List of doable items and get it delegated to yourself, learn 50 – 60 % of your boss work, create a Virtual Team to assist you.

4th **Mantra** "Read and learn a lot on your own".

Action Items: Know more than Your colleagues, Better Time management, Periodic self-review of the progress made.

5th Mantra "Maintain good Work Life balance".

Action Items: Follow "Rule of 100% presence", Separate a slice of time for your personal things at work place, maintain a "To do list" and an action item tracker, Develop a balanced and controlled mindset.

Made in the USA
Coppell, TX
10 January 2022